Sammie Crawford

Creating
WALL POCKETS

*10 gourd projects to paint
and hang*

Schiffer *Publishing Ltd*®

4880 Lower Valley Road · Atglen, PA 19310

To be an artist one must possess many gifts . . . absolute gifts,
which have not been acquired by one's own effort. This book is dedicated to my Lord,
Jesus Christ, who blessed me with the talent I have.

Important: To use your wall pocket to display fresh flower or plant arrangements, simply place a container inside to hold any needed water. The pocket alone is not waterproof!

Other Schiffer Books by the Author:

Painting Gourds with the Fairy Gourdmother®, ISBN 978-0-7643-4309-4

Building Gourd Birdhouses with the Fairy Gourdmother®, ISBN 978-0-7643-3736-9

Time for Gourds: 8 Clock Projects, ISBN 978-0-7643-3981-3

Other Schiffer Books on Related Subjects:

Miriam Joy's Wax Design Techniques, Miriam Joy, ISBN 978-0-7643-4467-1

Antler Art for Baskets and Gourds, Betsey Sloan, ISBN 978-0-7643-3615-7

Decorating Gourds: Carving, Burning, Painting, Sue Waters, ISBN 978-0-7643-1312-7

Published by Schiffer Publishing, Ltd.
4880 Lower Valley Road
Atglen, PA 19310
Phone: (610) 593-1777
Fax: (610) 593-2002
E-mail: Info@schifferbooks.com
Web: www.schifferbooks.com

Library of Congress Control Number: 2015957207

Cover design by Justin Watkinson
Type set in Affair/Bodoni MT
ISBN: 978-0-7643-5020-7

Printed in China

"Schiffer," "Schiffer Publishing, Ltd. and Design," and the "Design of pen and inkwell" are registered trademarks of Schiffer Publishing, Ltd.

For our complete selection of fine books on this and related subjects, please visit our website at www.schifferbooks.com. You may also write for a free catalog.

Schiffer Publishing's titles are available at special discounts for bulk purchases for sales promotions or premiums. Special editions, including personalized covers, corporate imprints, and excerpts, can be created in large quantities for special needs. For more information, contact the publisher.

We are always looking for people to write books on new and related subjects. If you have an idea for a book, please contact us at proposals@schifferbooks.com.

Contents

PREPARING THE *Gourd*

To create a wall pocket, the first step is to prepare the gourd.

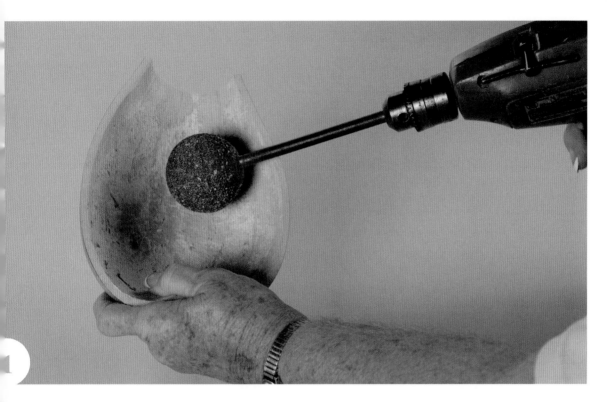

1 Cut the top off the gourd (approximately 2" to 3"), then cut it in half from top to bottom. Clean it out.

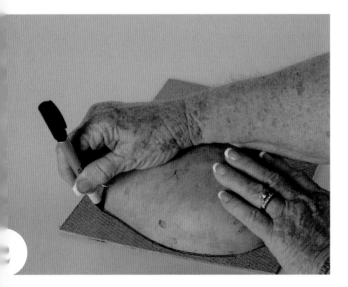

2 Place it on the plywood and draw around it.

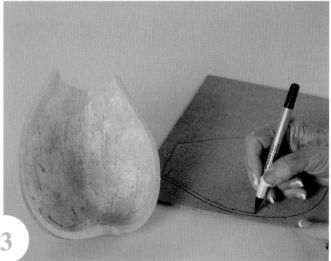

3 Allowing for the thickness of the gourd, draw a second line inside the first one.

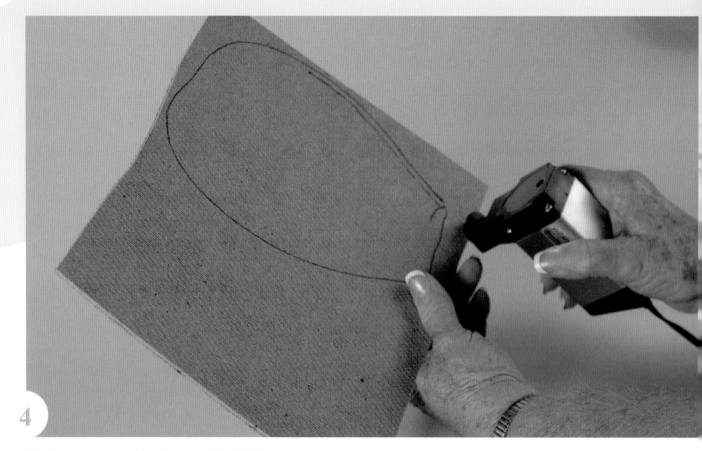

4

Cut the shape out using the second, inside line.

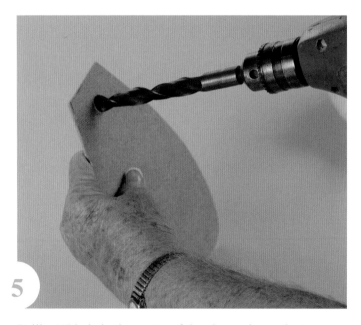

5

Drill a ¼" hole in the center of the plywood near the top.

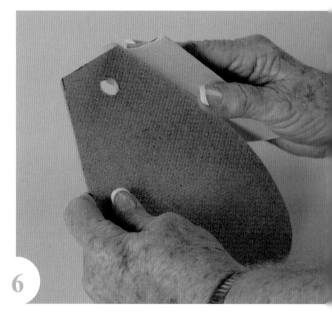

6

Sand the rough edges.

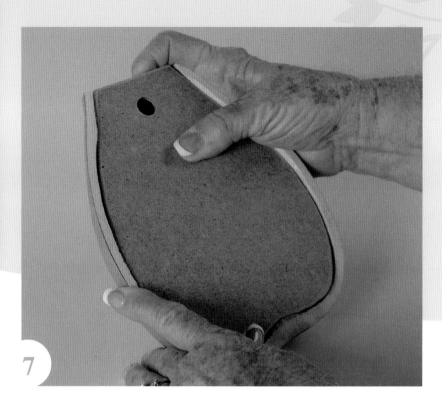

7

Sand or trim until the plywood fits nicely in the gourd; glue in place.

8

Fill the gaps with spackle and sand smooth when dry. Now you're ready to paint!

Last but not least... To protect your finished project, apply several light coats of spray varnish.
To use your wall pocket to display fresh flower or plant arrangements, simply place a container inside to
hold any needed water. The pocket alone is not waterproof!

Petroglyph WALL POCKET

PROJECT MATERIALS

PALETTE

DecoArt

Black

Russet

Slate Grey

Terra Cotta

White

BRUSHES

Loew-Cornell

Series 7000 #6 round

Series 7350 10/0 liner

SUPPLIES

10–11" tall pear-shaped gourd, blemish free

Craft saw

¼" plywood scrap

Wood glue

Drill and ¼" bit

Sandpaper

DAP Fast 'N Final Lightweight Spackling

Satin spray varnish

PAINTING THE DESIGN

See the next pages for *a closer look*

1. DO NOT PAINT THE GOURD. Apply the pattern.

2. Refer to the photo to know which horse is to be which color.

3. Use the liner brush and Black to outline all horses, to paint the manes, and to paint the handprints.

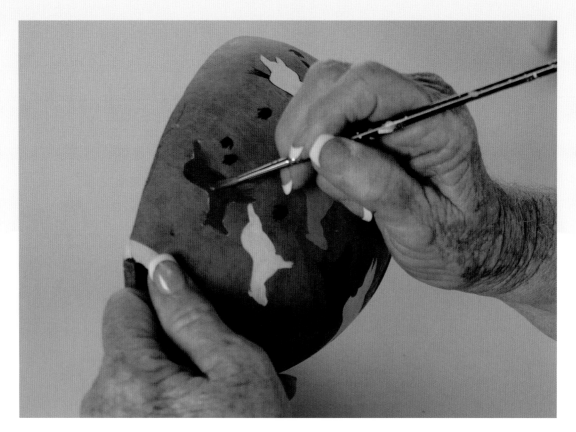

Paint the horses by referring to the photo for color placement.

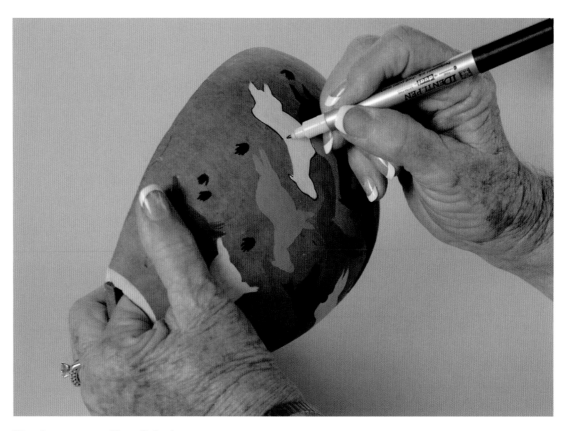

Use the pen to outline all the horses.

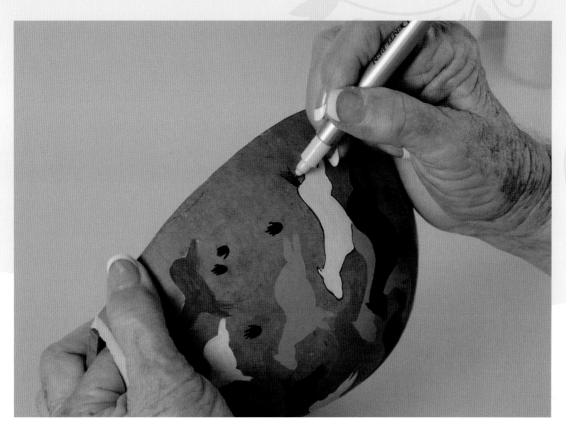

Use the pen to draw in the manes and tails on all horses.

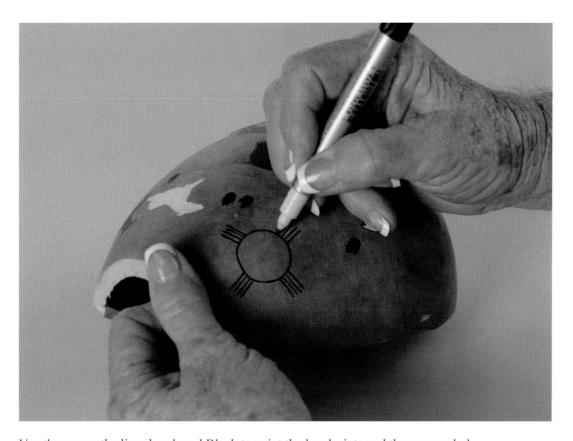

Use the pen or the liner brush and Black to paint the handprints and the sun symbol.

Faux Tooled Leather

WALL POCKET

PROJECT MATERIALS

PALETTE

DecoArt

Black

Rookwood Red

White

BRUSHES

Loew-Cornell

Series 7000 #4 round

Series 7300 #12 flat

Series 7350 10/0 liner

SUPPLIES

10–11" tall pear-shaped gourd, blemish free

Craft saw

¼" plywood scrap

Wood glue

Drill and ¼" bit

Sandpaper

DAP Fast 'N Final Lightweight Spackling

Leveling tool (optional)

Cosmetic sponge wedges

Memories Artprint Brown ink dye

Heat gun

Stylus

Brown shoe polish and brush

2 buttons

Glue

PAINTING THE DESIGN

See the next pages for *a closer look*

1. Paint the back of the gourd Rookwood Red.

2. Apply the oval rose pattern to the center of the gourd. Use the leveling tool to scribe a ¾" band across the middle.

3. You can scribe an optional band from one side to the other across the bottom. To do this, place your gourd on top of something that raises it to the level you need, and repeat the lines like the horizontal ones.

4. Paint the background in the oval Black using the #4 round brush. Use the liner brush and Black to outline the bands and center design.

5. Use the #12 brush and Black to shade the petals.

6. Use the sponge to apply the ink dye. Lightly pat to remove any streaks.

7. Use the heat gun to set the dye.

8. Use the stylus to place dots ¼" apart along both sides of the bands.

9. Use the liner brush and White for the stitches. If you start your stitch on one side of the dot and finish on the opposite side of the next one, it lends more interest than just painting a straight line from point A to point B.

10. When dry, apply brown shoe polish over the entire gourd (stitches too) and buff with the brush. No varnish is needed.

11. Clip off any shanks on the button backs and glue in place where the bands meet.

14

Apply pattern to center of the gourd and use the leveling tool to mark a band across the middle of the pocket.

Place the gourd on something to raise it up for marking the band that goes around the bottom from side to side. Apply the pattern.

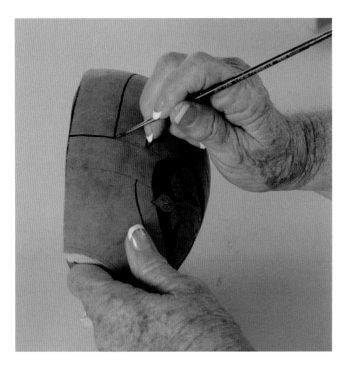

Use the round brush to paint the background inside the oval Black, and use the #12 flat to float on the rose petals. Use the liner brush to outline the bands in Black.

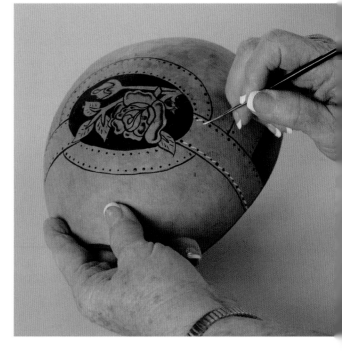

Use the stylus to make the Black dots, keeping them about ¼" apart. Use the liner brush and White to make the stitches.

Use the cosmetic sponge to apply the ink dye to the "leather" parts of the gourd. Do not dye the bands. Once the dye is applied, lightly pounce to remove any streaks.

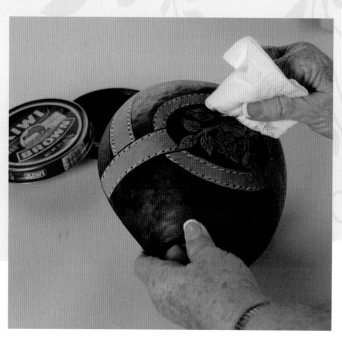

Apply brown shoe polish over the entire surface, including the stitches.

Use the heat gun to set the dye. Keep your hand near where you are heating. If it's too hot for your hand, it's too hot for the dye. Heat until it loses its shine.

Buff with a shoe brush. No need for varnish on this piece. If it ever gets dull, just buff it again like you would a shoe.

Eagle and Flag

WALL POCKET

PROJECT MATERIALS

PALETTE

DecoArt

Blue Violet

True Red

White

Prussian Blue

French Vanilla

Camel

Lt. Buttermilk

Golden Straw

Slate Grey

Soft Black

Rookwood Red

BRUSHES

Loew-Cornell

Series 7000 #6 round

Series 7300 #12 flat

Series 7350 10/0 liner

Series 7550 1" wash brush

SUPPLIES

10–11" tall pear-shaped gourd

Craft saw

¼" plywood scrap

Wood glue

Drill and ¼" bit

Sandpaper

DAP Fast 'N Final Lightweight Spackling

Blending gel

Satin spray varnish

PAINTING THE DESIGN

See the next pages for *a closer look*

. Basecoat the entire gourd White. Apply the pattern.

. Basecoat the flag with Blue Violet and True Red.

. Whitewash to give a weathered look. Do this several times if needed.

. Float a shadow by the partial stars and around the eagle's head with Prussian Blue.

. Float a shadow of Rookwood on the red stripes.

. Float a shadow of Slate on the white stripes.

. The beak is based French Vanilla, shaded with Camel.

. Use the blending gel and Lt. Buttermilk to highlight down the center of the beak.

9. The eyes are Golden Straw with Soft Black pupils and a Soft Black outline.

10. Float a little Soft Black around the eyes followed by a float of Slate Grey.

11. The feathers are Slate Grey done with the #12 flat and floats.

12. Use the liner brush to further add feathers along the edges.

Basecoat the entire gourd White. Paint the upper background Blue Violet, the stripes True Red, and the beak French Vanilla. Use the wash brush to wash it all with White.

Float Prussian Blue on the folds in the flag.

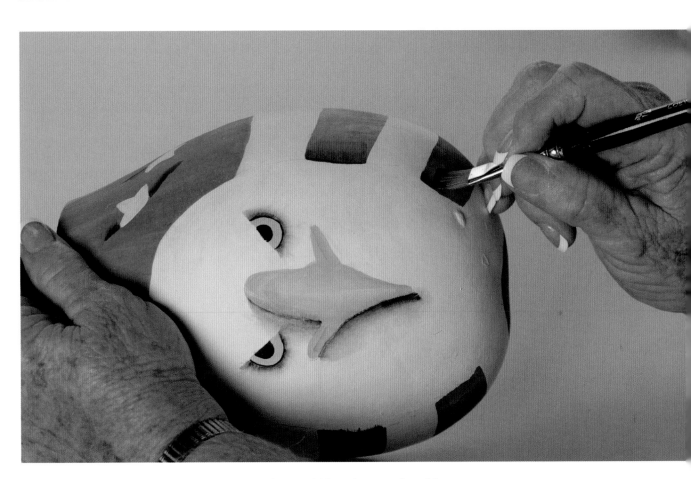

Float Rookwood against the bird on the red stripes and Slate Grey on the white ones.

Use the blending gel, then do a flip float of Lt. Buttermilk down the center of the beak.

Float around the outer edges of the beak with Camel. The eyes are Golden Straw.

Use the liner brush and Soft Black to outline the eyes and fill in the pupils.

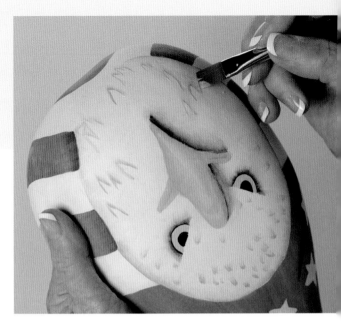

Do a wide float of Soft Black down the left side of the beak and around the eyes. Fill in the nostrils with Soft Black.

Use the #12 flat and Slate Grey for the feathers.

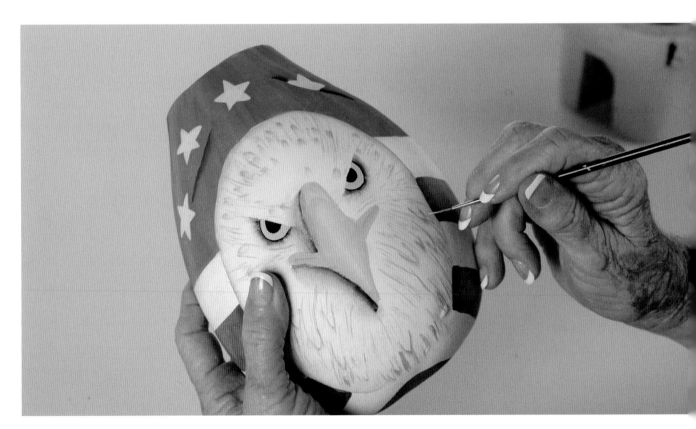

Use the same color and liner brush to add thin lines between the V's and along the edges. Leave the center of the forehead plain for highlight.

Place a White comma stroke in each eye for highlight.

Barrel WALL POCKET

PROJECT MATERIALS

PALETTE

DecoArt

Raw Sienna

Burnt Sienna

Copper Metallic

Emperor's Gold

BRUSHES

Loew-Cornell

Series 7300 #12 flat

Series 7350 10/0 liner

Series 7550 1" wash brush

SUPPLIES

10–11" tall pear-shaped gourd, blemish free

Craft saw

¼" plywood scrap

Wood glue

Drill and ¼" bit

Sandpaper

DAP Fast 'N Final Lightweight Spackling

Leveling tool

Chalk pencil

Satin spray varnish

PAINTING THE DESIGN

See the next pages for *a closer look*

There is no pattern needed for this beginner piece.

NOTE: The best way to ensure level lines is to stand your pocket up against a flat surface.

1. Use the leveling tool to scribe two 1½"–2" bands across the gourd. Basecoat them solid with Raw Sienna.

2. Use the wash brush to wash the rest of the gourd with a Raw Sienna wash.

3. When dry, draw a line from top to bottom in the center of the gourd. Use this as a guide for the rest of your lines. They will be narrower at the top and bottom because of the curvature of the gourd.

4. Use the liner brush and Burnt Sienna to make the wood grain pattern on each of the "boards." Wash with Burnt Sienna when finished.

5. Use the #12 flat and Copper metallic to paint the bands. Float Raw Sienna around the ends and add Emperor's Gold brads on the bands.

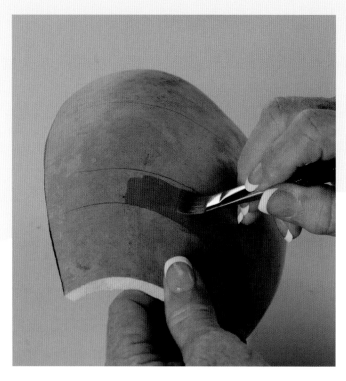

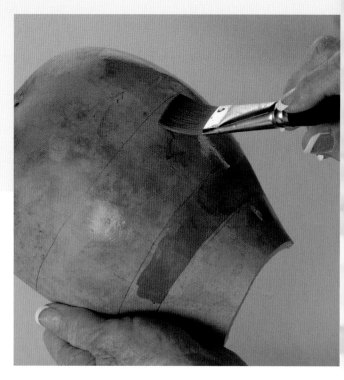

Use the leveling tool to scribe two 1½" bands across the gourd, and paint them Copper Metallic.

Wash the rest of the piece with Raw Sienna.

Use the chalk pencil to mark vertical lines. The staves will be narrower at the top and bottom due to the curvature of the gourd.

Use the liner brush and Burnt Sienna to make the woodgrain lines.
Wash the area with Burnt Sienna when finished.

Use the flat and Raw Sienna to make the "shadows"
at the ends of the bands.

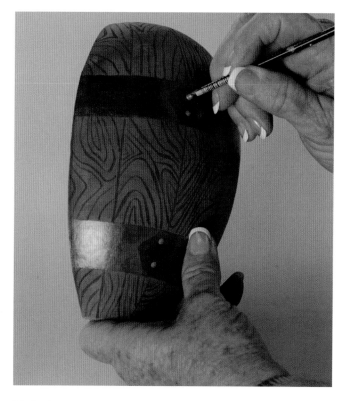

Make Emperor's Gold dots for the brads.

Tulip Basket WALL POCKET

PROJECT MATERIALS

PALETTE

DecoArt

French Vanilla

Burnt Umber

Honey Brown

White

Teal Green

Hauser Dk. Green (HDG)

Hauser Med. Green (HMG)

Hauser Lt. Green (HLG)

Spice Pink

Pink Chiffon

Raw Sienna

Colonial Green

Antique Mauve

Olive

BRUSHES

Loew-Cornell

Series 7000 #6 round

Series 7300 #12 flat

Series 7350 10/0 liner

SUPPLIES

10–11" tall pear-shaped gourd

Craft saw

¼" plywood scrap

Wood glue

Drill and ¼" bit

Sandpaper

DAP Fast 'N Final Lightweight Spackling

Blending gel

Satin spray varnish

PAINTING THE DESIGN

See the next pages for *a closer look*

1. Basecoat the whole piece with French Vanilla.

2. Apply the pattern and basecoat the basket Burnt Umber.

3. Basecoat the tulips Spice Pink.

4. Basecoat the leaves HMG.

5. Basecoat the ribbon with Colonial Green.

6. Use Raw Sienna and the round brush to make the reeds on the basket.

7. Use the #12 flat and Honey to highlight the reeds.

8. Shade the leaves with HDG.

9. Highlight the leaves with HLG.

10. Further highlight some of the leaf tips with Olive.

11. Shade the tulips with Antique Mauve.

12. Highlight with Pink Chiffon.

13. Use the liner brush and HLG for the stems.

14. Shade the ribbon with Teal Green.

15. Apply blending gel across the ribbon loops and do a flip float of a mix of Colonial Green and White, 1:1.

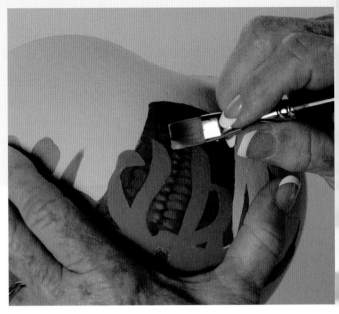

Basecoat the gourd French Vanilla, the basket Burnt Umber, the leaves Hauser Medium Green, the tulips Spice Pink, and the ribbon Colonial Green. Use the round brush and Raw Sienna to make the reeds on the basket.

Highlight the reeds using the flat and Honey.

Shade the tulips with Antique Mauve.

Highlight the tulips with Pink Chiffon.

Shade the leaves with Hauser Dark Green.

Highlight the leaves with Hauser Light Green. Further highlight using Olive.

The stems are also Hauser Light Green.

Shade the ribbon with Teal Green.

Apply blending gel across the ribbon loops and do a flip float
of the mix of Colonial Green and White, 1:1.

Birdhouse WALL POCKET

PROJECT MATERIALS

PALETTE

DecoArt

Lt. French Blue

Grey Sky

Hauser Dk. Green (HDG)

Hauser Med. Green (HMG)

Mint Julep

Lt. Avocado

Evergreen

Baby Pink

Royal Fuchsia

Honey

Milk Chocolate

Raw Umber

Marigold

White

Black

Antique White

French Grey Blue

BRUSHES

Loew-Cornell

Series 7000 #6 round

Series 7300 #12 flat

Series 7350 10/0 liner

SUPPLIES

10–11" tall pear-shaped gourd

Craft saw

¼" plywood scrap

Wood glue

Drill and ¼" bit

Sandpaper

DAP Fast 'N Final Lightweight Spackling

Blending gel

Satin spray varnish

34

PAINTING THE DESIGN

1. Basecoat the background Lt. French Blue; apply blending gel and add Grey Sky in patches. Mop to blend.

2. Base the leaves with HMG.

3. Shade the leaves with HDG and highlight with Mint Julep.

4. Base the roses Baby Pink.

5. Shade with Royal Fuchsia and highlight with a mix of Baby Pink and White, 1:1.

6. Base the birdhouse with Honey.

7. Shade with Milk Chocolate and highlight Marigold.

8. Shade under the left eave and inside the hole with Raw Umber.

9. Base the bird White.

10. Paint the head Black. Paint the tail and wing Grey Sky.

11. Shade under the wing with Antique White.

12. The "ghost" leaves are French Grey Blue.

13. The "ghost" roses are done the same as the others but using blending gel.

Sea Turtle WALL POCKET

PROJECT MATERIALS

PALETTE

DecoArt

Colonial Green

Indian Turquoise

Bleached Sand

Black Green

Bluegrass

Antique White

Mistletoe Green

Forest Green

Mulberry

Purple Cow

Mocha

Light Mocha

Lemon

Bright Green

Antique Gold

Soft Black

Country Blue

White

Black

Arbor Green

Mint Julep

Cocoa

BRUSHES

Loew-Cornell

Series 7000 #6 round

Series 7300 #12 flat

Series 7350 10/0 liner

SUPPLIES

10–11" tall pear-shaped gourd

Craft saw

¼" plywood scrap

Wood glue

Drill and ¼" bit

Sandpaper

DAP Fast 'N Final Lightweight Spackling

Sea sponge

Blending gel

Satin spray varnish

PAINTING THE DESIGN

NOTE: Undercoat all yellow fish with White first.

1. Basecoat entire gourd with Colonial Green.

2. The tall coral is Bleached Sand and Indian Turquoise, mixed 1:4, sponged over it.

3. The green coral is Mistletoe with Forest Green shading.

4. The purple coral is Mulberry with Purple Cow floated along the top edge.

5. The pink coral is Mocha with Light Mocha highlighting.

6. The sand is Antique White with Cocoa shading.

7. The kelp is Arbor Green with Mint Julep highlighting

8. The turtles are a mix of Black Green and Bluegrass, 1:1, with Antique White on the chest and Purple Cow touches on the flippers.

9. Add more Antique White to the mix for the highlighting and line work on the flippers.

10. Use this mix and blending gel to highlight the shell.

11. Darken that same mix by adding more Black Green to use for shading.

12. The yellow and green fish is Lemon with Bright Green fins and Antique Gold shading.

13. The yellow and black fish are Lemon with Soft Black and Antique Gold shading.

14. The yellow and blue fish is Country Blue and White and Black accents and Antique Gold shading.

15. The yellow fish with blue stripes is Country Blue and Lemon.

16. The Moorish idol fish is Black and White.

17. The bubbles are White floats with White comma strokes.

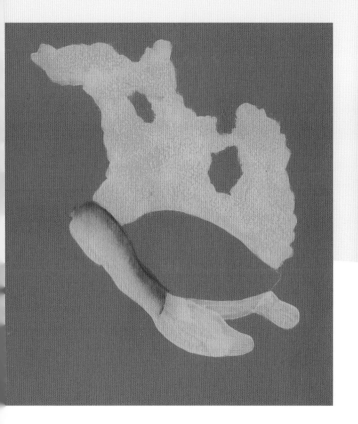

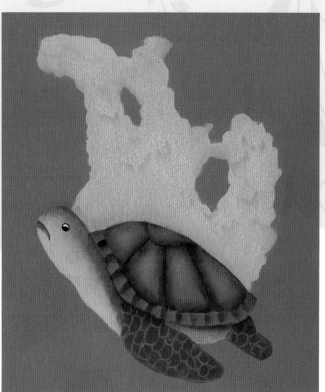

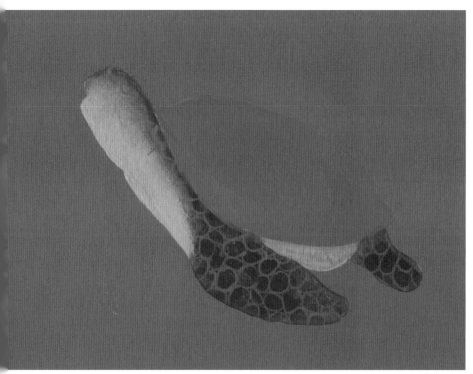

Rabbit WALL POCKET

PROJECT MATERIALS

PALETTE

DecoArt

Black

Graphite

Antique White

Lt. French Blue

Slate

Lt. Buttermilk

White

Terra Cotta

BRUSHES

Loew-Cornell

Series 7000 #6 round

Series 7300 #12 flat

Series 7350 10/0 liner

SUPPLIES

10–11" tall pear-shaped gourd

Craft saw

¼" plywood scrap

Wood glue

Drill and ¼" bit

Sandpaper

DAP Fast 'N Final Lightweight Spackling

Blending gel

Satin spray varnish

PAINTING THE DESIGN

See the next pages for *a closer look*

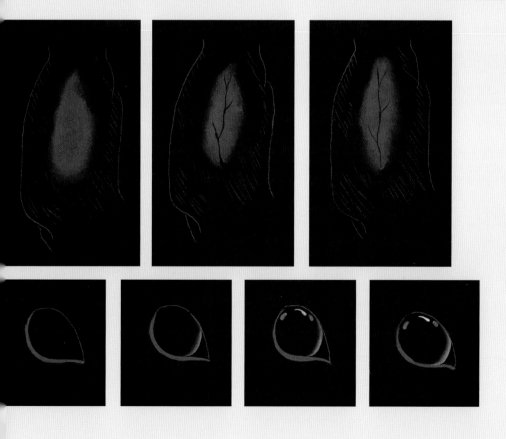

Basecoat the background Black and the rabbit Graphite; apply the pattern.

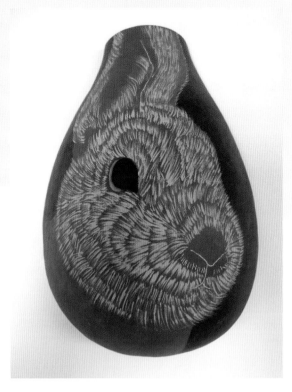

Use the liner brush and Slate for the first layer of fur. Use the same brush and Lt. French Blue for the second layer.

Use Antique White for the third layer.

Use Lt. Buttermilk for highlighting.

Use White to further enhance highlighting.

Apply blending gel and paint the inside of the ear with a mix of Terra Cotta and Lt. Buttermilk, 3:2.

Paint the eye solid Black and add a White comma stroke and a large C stroke around the edge of the eye. Use Black for the lashes. Use the liner brush and White for the whiskers.

Merry Christmas

Candy Jar WALL POCKET

PROJECT MATERIALS

PALETTE

DecoArt

Pansy Lavender

Black Plum

Lilac

Spiced Pumpkin

Georgia Clay

True Red

Winter Blue

White

Banana Cream

Golden Straw

Hauser Lt. Green (HLG)

Hauser Med. Green (HMG)

Hauser Dk. Green (HDG)

Terra Coral

Jack-O-Lantern

Raw Sienna

Emperor's Gold

Cadmium Orange

Honey

Silver Sage

Cool White

Camel

BRUSHES

Loew-Cornell

Series 700 #4 round

Series 7300 #12 flat

Series 7350 10/0 liner

#275 ½" mop brush

SUPPLIES

10–11" tall gourd

Craft saw

¼" plywood scrap

Wood glue

Drill and ¼" bit

Sandpaper

DAP Fast 'N Final Lightweight Spackling

Blending gel

Satin spray varnish

44

PAINTING THE DESIGN

No basecoat needed. Apply the pattern.

(Use the mop brush to soften shading and highlighting.)

1. **Gumballs:**
   Purple: Pansy Lavender base, Black Plum shade, Lilac highlight
   Orange: Spiced Pumpkin, Georgia Clay
   Red: True Red, Black Plum, White
   Yellow: Banana Cream and Cool White, 3:2 mix; Golden Straw
   Green: HMG base, HDG shade, HLG highlight
   Fireballs: True Red, Black Plum, Terra Coral stripes

   Candy canes:
   Red: White with True Red stripes, Black Plum shade, Winter Blue shade on white parts, White thin line down center for shine
   Green: HMG base, HDG shade, HLG highlight, Winter Blue on white parts, White thin line down center

2. **Peppermints:**
   Painted the same as the red and green canes.

   Pillow candies:
   Yellow: Banana Cream and Cool White, 3:2 mix; True Red and White stripes, Golden Straw shade
   Green: HLG, True Red and White stripes, HDG shade

3. **Fruit slices:**
   Green: HLG base, HDG shade.
   Yellow: Banana Cream and Cool White, 3:2 mix, base; Golden Straw shade
   Orange: Spiced Pumpkin base, Georgia Clay shade

4. **Hard candies:**
   Wreath: Jack-O-Lantern and Camel, 3:2 mix for stripes; with Raw Sienna shade, HMD wreath, True Red bow

   Tree: HMG edges and tree, HDG shade and outline

   Star: True Red star, Jack-O-Lantern and Camel, 3:2 mix for stripes; Winter Blue shade

   Holly: True Red edges and berries, HDG leaves, Black Plum shade.

5. **Ribbon candy:**
   True Red, HMG stripes, Winter Blue shade, White flip float across center for shine.

6. **Bow:**
   True Red base. Apply blending gel across the center of ribbon loops, and do a flip float of Cadmium Orange highlight. Shade with Black Plum, and use liner brush to edge the ribbon with Emperor's Gold.

   Berries:
   Same.

   Holly leaf:
   HMG, HDG, HLG

   Gold ball:
   Honey undercoat, Emperor's Gold base, floats of red and green plus a White comma stroke

7. **Gift tag:**
   Soft Sage basecoat, HMG border, Black lettering, Emperor's Gold cord.

Santa WALL POCKET

PROJECT MATERIALS

PALETTE

DecoArt

Tomato Red

Black Plum

Cocoa

Antique White

Lt. Buttermilk

Medium Flesh

Cadmium Red

White

Gingerbread

Heritage Brick

Payne's Grey

Deep Midnight

Black

French Grey Blue

Dark Chocolate

Hi-Lite Flesh

BRUSHES

Loew-Cornell

Series 7000 #4 round

Series 7300 #2, 12 flats

Series 7300 #12 flat

Series 7350 10/0 liner

Series 7520 ½" filbert rake

#275 ½" mop brush

SUPPLIES

10–11" tall pear-shaped gourd

Craft saw

¼" plywood scrap

Wood glue

Drill and ¼" bit

Sandpaper

DAP Fast 'N Final Lightweight Spackling

Sea sponge

Blending gel

Satin spray varnish

PAINTING THE DESIGN

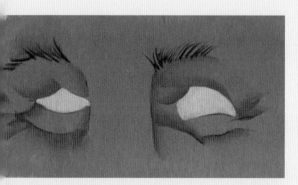
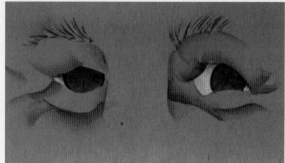
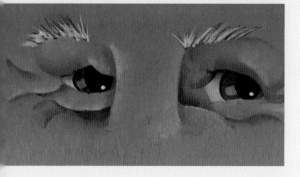

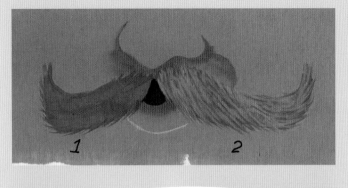
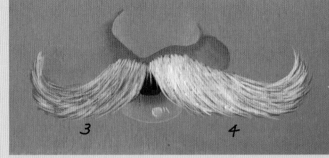

PAINTING THE DESIGN

1. Basecoat the background with Payne's Grey in a choppy pattern. Don't try to get it even or solid because it won't show later.

2. Sponge Deep Midnight all over the Grey.

3. Float French Blue Grey along the profile, fading away from the face.

4. Wash with Deep Midnight when dry.

5. Basecoat the face with Medium Flesh, the hat with Tomato Red, and the fur and hair with Cocoa. Again don't worry about getting a smooth solid coat on the fur and hair because it won't show.

6. Apply pattern details and shade the face with Gingerbread, deepening some shadows with Heritage Brick. Highlight with Hi-Lite Flesh. Refer to the photo for placement. Fill the mouth in with Heritage Brick.

7. Paint the eyes with Lt. Buttermilk. The irises are French Grey Blue with Black pupils. Float Deep Midnight across the eyeball under the eyelid fading downward.

8. Use the liner brush and Deep Midnight to outline the irises very thinly and pull radiating lines from the pupil outward. Use the #2 flat and White to place a shine in the eye and then a White dot.

9. The eyebrows are first Dark Chocolate, then Antique White and finally White. Less is more so don't get carried away. Leave a little of each color showing.

10. Shade the cap with Black Plum and highlight with Cadmium Red. Use several coats if needed to get a good highlight.

11. Use the filbert rake and Antique White for the first layer of color on the beard and fur. Patience is the secret of a good beard, so don't take any shortcuts. Use Lt. Buttermilk next and finally White for the lightest highlights. Note that the fur is made with shorter strokes than the hair.

12. Paint the bells on the cap White and apply blending gel. Then float Payne's Grey across the top of the bell, Antique White on one side, and Tomato Red on the other; mop to blend. The holes are Black.

Patterns
PETROGLYPH

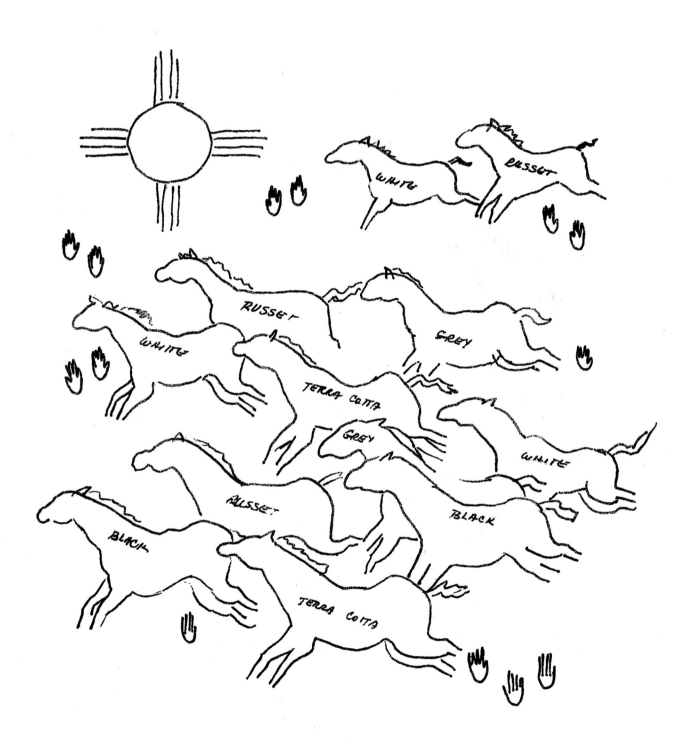

FAUX TOOLED
LEATHER

(Enlarge pattern 125% for full size)

EAGLE AND FLAG

(Enlarge pattern 200% for full size)

(No pattern needed for the BARREL project)

TULIP BASKET

BIRDHOUSE

(Enlarge pattern 125% for full size)

SEA TURTLE

(Enlarge pattern 125% for full size)

RABBIT

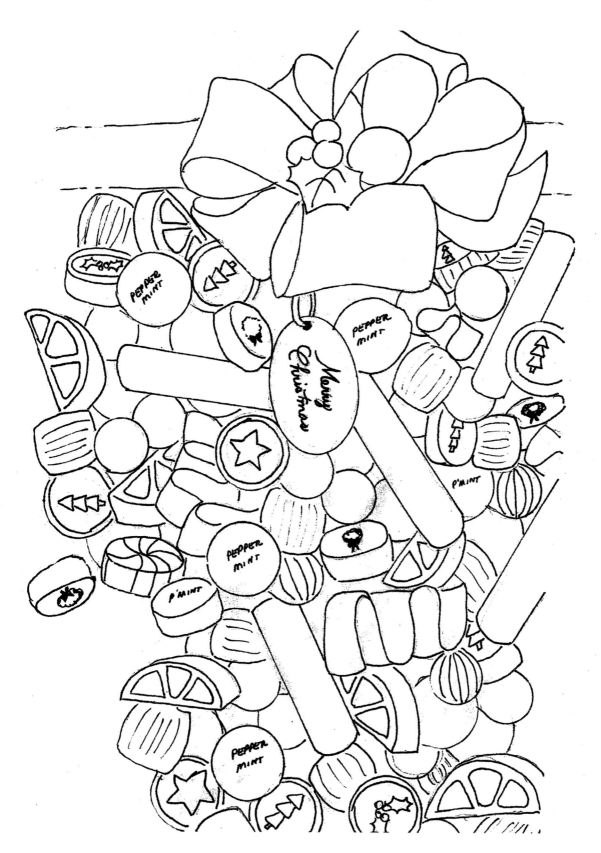

CANDY JAR

(Enlarge pattern 125% for full size)

SANTA

(Enlarge pattern 125% for full size)